Microcosm Publishing is Portland's most diversified publishing house and distributor, with a focus on the colorful, authentic, and empowering. Our books and zines have put your power in your hands since 1996, equipping readers to make positive changes in their lives and in the world around them. Microcosm emphasizes skill-building, showing hidden histories, and fostering creativity through challenging conventional publishing wisdom with books and bookettes about DIY skills, food, bicycling, gender, self-care, and social justice. What was once a distro and record label started by Joe Biel in a drafty bedroom was determined to be *Publishers Weekly*'s fastest-growing publisher of 2022 and #3 in 2023, and is now among the oldest independent publishing houses in Portland, OR, and Cleveland, OH. We are a politically moderate, centrist publisher in a world that has inched to the right for the past 80 years.

IT'S ALL GRIST FOR THE MILL

Have you ever gone through a devastating, confusing, and heartbreaking breakup? Well, the truth is, we all have and will. Endings are more likely to happen than not, so why don't we accept it and teach each other how to get through them, causing as little harm to ourselves and others as one can? The Heartbreak Guide is meant to help you reframe your romantic life by dragging it back out of the clouds, down to the earth, and away from the fantastical love stories we were raised to expect. Through the use of Object Relations Theory, you will begin to understand that an even bigger story beyond any of your breakups is actually unfolding; *the journey of you finding yourself.*

The purpose of this zine is to help you develop a more empathic and realistic framework to view your romantic life and your breakups. The perspective that our society has fed us about romantic relationships and love is unrealistic, sometimes toxic, and can leave us vulnerable to a feeling of disappointment when a relationship ends. Through the act of reading this zine, you should be better able to communicate with partners and, although heartbreaking at times, feel a sense of empowerment when a romantic relationship ends because you spoke your truth, and know at your core that they are just not the right person for you.

This is where things may feel difficult to swallow—the harsh truth if you will. We are taught to seek love and then to make it work forever and in perpetuity. Throw poetic tantrums to hold on to the objects of our affection. I'm going to ask you to take a step back and look at this pointillistic painting of people and emotions we exist in. If you believe in lifelong partnership, it's only supposed to work out once in monogamy and very few times with polyamory. The odds are against you.

There is no right answer to what a relationship "should" look like or how it "should" function. Relationships, like people, are far too complex and nuanced for a list of generic steps and solutions to your struggles, confusion, and frustrations. This zine is meant to spur self-reflection on your own wants and needs, to learn how to clearly communicate them to your partner(s), and finally (this is where we struggle as a society) *accept when these fundamental aspects are not aligning with our own wants and needs.*

It is truly a beautiful experience to be cared for as a whole-ass human beyond just an attempt at romance. To have clear communication on wants, needs, and expectations for romantic relationships helps to remove the sense that a simple mismatch is a personal attack. We all have needs and expectations but by not going through the process of building insight we cannot clearly articulate them to others. Without thinking critically about yourself, the unconscious drives that want to be satisfied can present themselves in behaviors related to our interpersonal relationships, some of which can be maladaptive and unintentionally harmful to both ourselves and our partners.

What if you could shift your perspective? Expect to feel heartbroken from time to time because relationships will run their course? Understand that your past partner is a flawed human on their own life journey, not a villain of rejection? Be able to reflect on how a relationship helped you grow rather than feel your time was wasted? The initial consent to a relationship dynamic, however defined, is not a guarantee. There is always a risk of feeling painful emotions when a relationship comes to its conclusion. This is the price we pay for rolling the relationship dice. If the house has the advantage, isn't it best to at least know the odds before you bet? Lay it all out on the table and see where you align and where you differ? Compromise if you can, and walk away with your pride if you can't?

In the following pages, I will discuss object relations theory in order to help understand our psychological drive towards love and partnership. This theory is a branch of psychoanalytic theory that focuses on relationships being crucial to personality development and our understanding of interpersonal relationship dynamics. My hope is that with this knowledge, you can reduce the trauma and devastation that often accompanies breakups, and even use them as a tool to learn and grow.

ENDINGS, LOSS, AND TRANSITIONS

I can understand if your first impression of this zine's perspective is one of pessimism, but it's not. It's an attempt to teach you the psychological drive towards love and partnership, why breakups are not only common but psychologically painful, and holds the perspective that the relationships we build throughout our lives reflect, influence, and directly correlate to our personal self-growth.

This is an attempt to shift your perspective from the rom-com we were raised to anticipate to an understanding that relationships over a lifespan are more experimentation than clearly defined steps one must follow to find success. Life itself is a process. If met with curiosity, all the good, bad, and neutral moments can begin to expose patterns over time. Areas within us that need focus, attention, and care can begin to be examined with openness. Shifts can start to happen with intent. Accept that one was not born with all the skills needed. Just like when learning a trade, it takes years of experience and mistakes to truly become a master craftsman. And like it or not, your emotions are the fundamental tools in your belt. So, go out, make all the mistakes, have the most fun, fall in love, be in the moment, but let's also be kind to each other when we outgrow one another.

Endings, loss, transition, and change are very difficult for most. In therapy we call ending a relationship with a patient"termination." Therapists know that when treatment is coming to an end clients can act out, symptoms that had improved can return, anger towards the therapist can surface, and some clients just stop coming before the actual end date. I call this getting "professionally ghosted" and it can look a lot like a traditional breakup. None of it is personal, it's more about the emotions the client is feeling about losing a supportive relationship, even if it's because they have met their goals.

Even if you're the one ending a relationship you will still experience the emotional loss of a breakup. We act out, we get cold, and we want to explain the emotional pain by devaluing the other or making them out to be the villain of our story. If we feel hurt, then it must be someone's fault. We begin to pinpoint and ruminate on moments that now feel like personal attacks. (Abuse and intentional harm are not related to this point. Causing harm to others is a hard no for me.) The reality is that a breakup is a triggering event that stirs up old wounds that we may not even be aware of on a conscious level. This connection to the past experiences we have had, but are unaware of, fully creates an intensified emotional experience in relation to our partners in the present.

No matter what you do, you will still experience all the painful emotions we humans love to avoid. But I believe they exist for a reason. It would be naïve to think a naturally occurring phenomenon within our bodies could simply be ignored or avoided without consequence. They hold power, they drive us and shape us from birth to death. Shouldn't one explore what they have to offer? What if you could face a painful emotional experience while knowing it's just another human-ass experience you can endure and find new knowledge within?

Feel your feelings. Express them, but don't use them to retaliate or harm others. Don't be afraid of them (emotional states will not last forever if released), in fact avoiding them, numbing them, or repressing them will actually limit the ability to feel and access all emotions. The continuum of emotions that exists within us are tied together. They all have equal value and purpose; to lock away one set locks them all away. Avoiding painful, uncomfortable emotions will also reduce joy, happiness, and excitement. Numbing and avoidance reduce one's ability to create meaningful relationships with others, because in order to do so we must be vulnerable.

I'm not trying to give the impression that by reading this you'll never feel the pain and sadness that comes with a breakup. You will. I'm also not advertising a way to be friends with all your past partners. The romantic interest or partner-to-friend pipeline is not always a smooth or clear transition. Some people need time away before coming back into the fold of your life. Some may slowly reemerge after some random public run-ins. Some you may never see or talk to again. What's important to take away is the understanding of the psychological dynamics that can occur to reframe the experience and the breakup itself. This is to benefit you as you move forward in the healing process.

The emotional reality that comes with endings is difficult for most. To leave the house that the relationship built standing would mean we may have to reflect upon this monument in the future. To burn it down and build a new house with fresh walls and paint, we may successfully avoid looking at ourselves in relation to what once stood. Each relationship we create is like a mile marker in our lives. They represent who we were, what we thought we wanted, what we didn't know, and the mistakes that we made. Sometimes these things don't seem to hold much meaning until we get further down the highway of time, and we encounter something unexpected. Suddenly the past now makes sense in the present.

Fear of self-reflection keeps us building new houses on the same foundation and expecting different outcomes. We keep falling into the same patterns and dynamics with different people hoping to find success and that change will just occur. It won't. It's what is known, what is familiar. Even if these dynamics are unhealthy, there is a sense of comfort in the repetition. The only way to break a pattern is to reflect on why it exists and how it is connected to ourselves. Insight gives birth to new options and paths. This is a brave act.

I personally prefer my metaphorical streets lined with old houses I no longer inhabit but can revisit to connect to my present. Relationship outcomes are precarious because it involves two individuals: two complex emotional worlds making themselves known through our behavior. You can have friends who you once dated and also be the villain in some of the narratives held by others. We can learn from mistakes and take accountability when we unintentionally cause harm, but we can't shift someone's mindset to fit the narrative we think they should hold.

Breakups are loss. You need to grieve the reality you had known, as well as what you had envisioned in your future. It is normal for your mind to run through, on repeat, what went wrong, what could have been different, what you may have missed, and thoughts about what your ex partner may be doing. They took up a section of your mind for some time, they were a part of your day to day. But the one thing you can do is remind yourself that although this feels abnormal, it is a normal reaction to loss. Expressing it honestly is the only way for grief to work its magic.

OBJECT RELATIONS THEORY

Okay my armchair psychoanalysts, this is where we will dive into theory. Let's start with the psychoanalytic concept most people have heard of: *The Unconscious.* I often use the phrase "physical metaphor" to describe behavioral patterns because our behaviors are a representation of our internal worlds in the physical. If you ever took a psychology 101 course, I'm sure you have seen the iceberg image used to represent the unconscious, but I feel this image is lacking because it does not explain the connection and interplay the unconscious has with how we navigate the world.

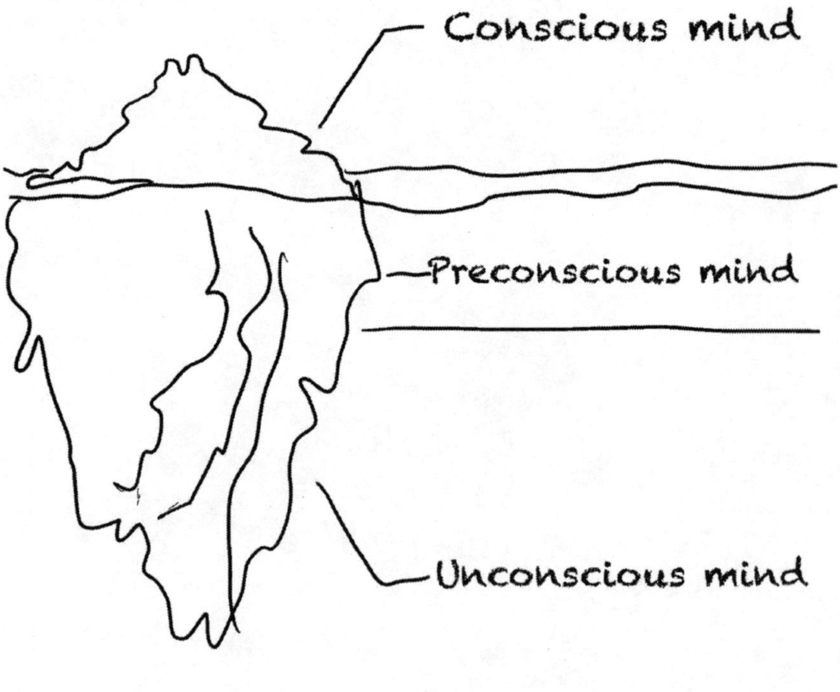

I would like to share my own visual metaphor to help you better understand the foundation of my theoretical beliefs.

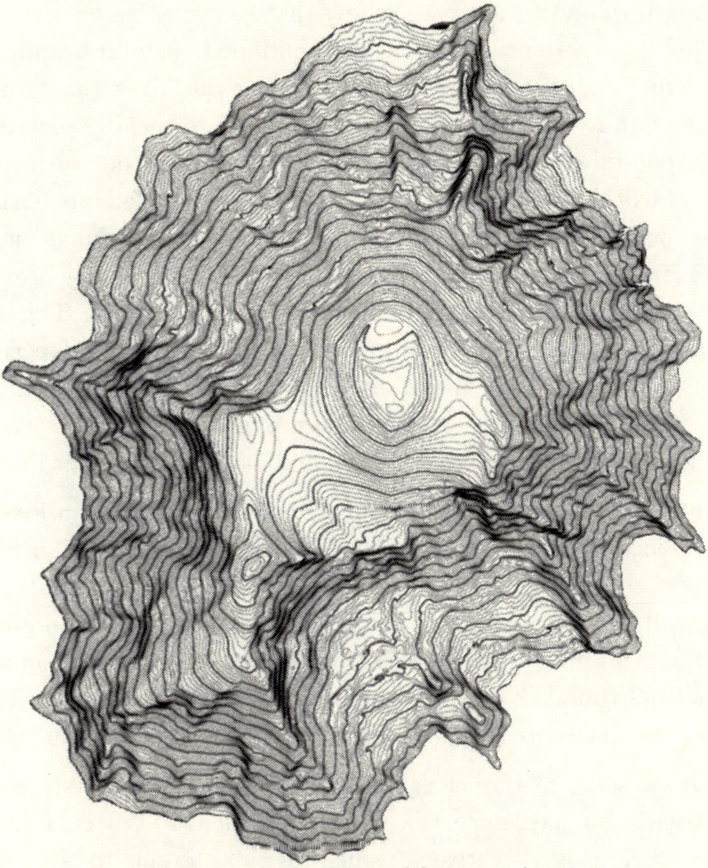

The Topographical Map of the Unconscious

The violent act of a tectonic shift creates mountains. We are aware of this on some level, but we don't judge the mountain for its traumatic birth. We build paths to get over, around, and through. We romanticize the bravery it takes to climb to the top. We notice the juxtaposition to other natural features and paint the landscape. People are full of emotional mountains birthed out of pain only to enter the physical world through behavior. Understanding their origins can help us be able to step back and take ourselves fully into view.

Our behavioral patterns represent the tips of these emotional mountains. The therapist's skill set allows them to help define and bring into focus this topographical map of the unconscious. Everything that sits on the surface could only exist with the support of what lies beneath. It's not good or bad, right or wrong. It just is.

In psychoanalytic theory we believe that everyone has an unconscious which holds experiences from early childhood, painful traumas, and various emotional wounds we obtain during our lives that can cause us to play out a wide range of patterns related to seeking pleasure and avoiding painful emotions. When we are unaware of our own internal emotional worlds we run the risk of repeating the maladaptive patterns. These experiences are what sit at the base of an emotional mountain peak. This can make a breakup not just about this particular breakup. It becomes about all the wounds this ending now represents. This ending is happening in the present but emotionally you are also experiencing the past. It is through the act of making the unconscious conscious and feeling the painful emotions related to our experiences that we can begin to gain insight, heal, and live healthier, and dare I say, happier lives.

The pain of a breakup is the emotional experience of a loss of an object, "object" meaning the internalized experience of a relationship with an external thing or person. When a relationship ends it not only ends in the physical sense, but we must also end it internally and mentally. This is terrifying for most. This internalized experience of love and safety helps us feel grounded, accepted, and whole. When we lose this, it causes us to become disoriented and it takes time to readjust and heal.

To make sense of ourselves and feel stable in our identities, we must connect with our past experiences and link them to our current life in the present. This is a creative act since we must be able to both imagine the experiences in our mind and then communicate them to another. I'm sorry to say that the process that leads us to feeling congruent within ourselves is not free. There is no clearly defined set of steps or rules to follow to get there. The price of self-growth is experiencing all the pain and sadness that comes with it. There can also be loss in this process. You may outgrow relationships, friendships, comfortable patterns of being, and coping mechanisms. All of it is sad and necessary at the same time.

To be able to understand how we develop our interpersonal patterns of behavior, we can begin to build insight into how we have been approaching and perceiving our romantic lives. This insight can allow us to shift the narrative to one that is more reflective of who we are and how we see partnership fitting into the life we want to create for ourselves. Object relations theory sort of sprung out of psychoanalytic when theorists were starting to study infant and childhood development. Would it be rather bold of me to state that our way of relating to others, building relationships, and our ability to experience love and emotional safety is fundamentally rooted in our experience as infants? Well, I am.

Everything about us as humans is meant for survival. When we have a traumatic experience or one that brings emotional discomfort, it is as though our body and mind want to defend it from happening again. Although terribly complex and amazing, it is also a flawed system that can overcorrect and misjudge. Our early infantile pre-verbal experiences get this process started and determine how we start to engage with the world as we gain autonomy. To help you visualize what I mean by this, I think talking about art therapy for a moment could be beneficial.

When working with clients through the use of art and art process I like to tell them that the finished product should not be the focus. The expectation of needing to create a masterpiece derails creativity. Each image made is just a stepping-stone to the next, which could not have been made without the artwork that came prior. Every time we engage in making art we are learning, we are making mistakes, we gain inspiration to inform our next piece, and so on. This is reflective of our own personal growth. The journey requires every experience and misstep that has led us into this very moment and informs us as we move forward in time. Applying this developmentally, the way in which your parent(s) were able (or unable) to meet your needs as an infant is reflected in the way you approach relationships today.

The complexity of this developmental process is due to the reality that our parents are inherently flawed humans playing out their own interpersonal behavioral patterns with us. The way in which our parents were parented influenced their parenting, and so on. If one were to look back at their family tree trends would likely appear. Biology, epigenetics, environment, and behavior all have an influence, and we cannot change our biology or genes and we cannot choose our environment as children. Understanding object relations theory in this context is essential to creating the life we want.

The following sections will cover the developmental process of moving from infancy to obtaining "object constancy" in childhood. All of which will be explained and then related to how this sets us up to develop the attraction we have to certain types of dynamics within our relationships as adults, and how we deal with breakups and heartbreak.

The Symbiotic Phase:

In the womb, every need for survival and safety was fulfilled automatically without having to cry out or signal. This is known as "the blissful state," which some theorists believe we are trying to return to in some way by seeking a romantic partner. As infants enter the reality of the world through birth, they will first spend about six months in what Margaret Mahler, one of the main theorists in the development of object relations, called the "symbiotic phase." In this phase they are still fused with a parent psychologically and cannot tell what is them and what is not because they have not gained the awareness that they exist separately from their parent. They have yet to recognize that a world outside of this fused relationship exists.

Separation-Individuation:

Hatching Sub-Phase:

The process of growing up is one of moving from total fusion and dependence with our parent in the womb, to independence in the world centered within our sense of self. Mahler developed the term "separation-individuation" for a phase that begins as we start to realize we exist separately from our parent. What a trip that moment must be. The first sub-phase involving the recognition of self is known as "hatching." There are many factors that play into this, but I think the illusion of this fused state begins to deteriorate simply due to both the infant's physical development and the parent's inability to consistently meet the baby's needs with the same immediacy that made it feel as though the baby was magically doing it themselves. At this point, most parents have gone months without proper sleep; can you really blame them for any delays? This recognition of the self also starts off the internal conflict that will occur as we struggle to understand that our parent(s) are not in fact the idealized perfect parent we experienced within the symbiotic phase.

Practicing Sub-Phase:

We soon start to develop the motor skills that will lunge us into exploring the early stages of our autonomy. Mahler called this sub-phase "practicing," and it begins as we transition into toddlerhood. The boundaries of what is good and what is bad is reflected to us from our parent(s). Their perception of the world, what they feel is normal, and their own anxieties start to seep in and shape our interactions with our environment and with others. What is reflected to us on how we should engage with the world around us starts to create the ways in which we think we should act.. If these concepts are at odds with our core self, internal conflicts will arise.

Rapprochement Sub-Phase:
The final sub-phase is called "rapprochement," which involves a kind of push and pull between wanting to be independent but also feeling anxious we will lose our parent if we do explore. The difference between this phase and the one prior is the sense of fear of what will happen when independence is reached. This is when the child will run off but look back to confirm the parent is still present and watching. The child sometimes seems hellbent on exploration one moment and then the next they are clinging to their parent's leg. Separation anxiety can develop if the child experiences some type of repetitive failure when they return to seek their parent to receive this comfort. They can feel lost, abandoned, or forgotten. This phase happens before they have developed what is called "object constancy," which is the ability to hold the image, memory, and internalized sense of the parent within themselves. This internalization grounds them and keeps a connection to the comfort and safety they once could only obtain by being in the presence of their parent.

What occurs between parent and child during these sub-phases within separation- individuation are what determine how the child will internalize the parent when they do reach object constancy. There is also an internal struggle for children at this time where they are trying to make sense of the fact that their parent is not the "all good" parent they experienced in the fused state. It can be confusing and hurtful. Any missteps our parents made, as well intentioned as they were, hurt us because we could not fully comprehend the reality and depth of why these mistakes occurred.

These upsetting experiences stuck with us, we started to behave in ways to avoid feeling the discomfort again, and if we were successful in finding a way to avoid it, we continued to repeat the strategy. The patterns that were successful in keeping us emotionally and physically safe during childhood may now be maladaptive as adults, which is why looking back to how they developed can help us shift them or release them.

I discussed the precarious nature of childhood development to highlight the different relationship dynamics we are bringing into a partnership. It's when these ingrained concepts end up being in opposition or out of alignment with our partner's that they can lead to difficulty, tension, and breakups. By reflecting on your own unique childhood experiences and how the complexities of the dynamics have shaped your patterns in your present life, it becomes easier to see, accept, and show empathy towards others you build relationships with. *We are all just messy-ass kids dressed up in adult suits trying to get our needs met while making out with each other. We are flawed, and we are trying.*

Interpersonal Romantic Relationships:

So now that we have zoomed in on specific phases within our development and zoomed out to see how vast and complex the influences of each are, I'd like to refocus on how this is playing out within our romantic relationships as adults. Object constancy of our original object, our parent, is what satisfies the internal need to feel loved and safe, but rather than requiring our parent to be with us, it's like ordering a drink at a bar in New Orleans: we can take it to go. Our experience of this is likely limited to the specific type of love and security our parent(s) were able to provide, even if we recognize these shortcomings as an adult.

When we fall in love or become emotionally attached to someone, they become an "internalized object." When we internalize a romantic interest as a love object it recreates the sense of love and safety that our internalized parent(s) once could only provide. When we are unsure of the security around the dynamic we can start to feel anxious. Without clear direct communication about the boundaries within a relationship we can get confused and overly excited to feel this comfort the potential object holds. We can over commit to those who aren't looking for commitment, we can feel surprised when what is displayed in real life doesn't match the version we hold internally, and if you have ever seen the show *Catfish*, we can trick ourselves into being in love with a photo of someone we aren't even talking to. People often say their partners make them feel "whole," but what I think this feeling is actually referring to is the ability to have someone as this internalized object.

If our understanding of what being loved is like is tied to our parents, then the repetitive patterns we play out within our romantic relationships are ones of familiarity and recognition of what is already known. Unfortunately, sometimes these patterns do not serve us positively and end up triggering our old wounds. There is an innate attraction to dynamics we unconsciously recognize even if they are unhealthy, because we already know how to navigate and exist within that dynamic. In psychoanalysis, this is known as "Repetition compulsion," where one may unconsciously seek out interpersonal dynamics that reflect those from their past. Not only that, but we've dealt with it before and have strategies in place. The unknown can seem like more of a risk.

When you think back to the relationship dynamics you have experienced, do you notice any common themes? Emotional states within them that you have experienced that are similar? Ways your partners made you feel? Ways of interacting or communicating that repeat? Any common trends in how you treated partners or ways they have treated you? By asking ourselves these types of questions we can better identify possible dynamics we are unconsciously attracted to.

Society reinforces this idea that one day we will suddenly have our own quirky-meet-cute and then our forever life in love will begin to unfold. What is lacking from this concept of love conquering all is the education on direct authentic communication, interpersonal relational skills, emotional intelligence and maturity, boundaries, wants, needs, and expectations. All of which are fundamental in taking this feeling of love and turning it into a long-term satisfying relationship for both or all partners. The pursuit of finding our other half, this blissful state, is setting us up to feel disappointment. Your partner(s) will not know or be able to meet your needs unless you have insight into what they are and then are able to clearly articulate them.

Nancy McWilliams, a psychoanalytic theorist and writer, states that we can all access a natural process of self-understanding and psychological maturation. Just like the early psychological developmental phases in childhood we covered, we can take ourselves further and gain a higher level of emotional maturity through the self in adulthood. It doesn't matter if you want to find a partner to marry and have kids with or if you are only interested in casual hookups where you, with consent, take Polaroids of their feet. There are people out there who will want what you do, but without a healthy understanding of these processes many find it difficult to articulate what they are looking for and why. This can cause us to commit to the first lust-filled connection we find and then feel confused when it fades or blows up in a ball of flames.

The purpose of all this is to leave you with a lot of questions for yourself because you are the only one with the answers. The difficulties of your dating life fall solely within yourself. There is no judgment or blame here; it's just reality. You only have control to change your own patterns, not your partner's, and thus hopefully change the type of partners you seek with the insight you have gained. Just because you want someone to want you and the type of relationship you can clearly envision with them, does not mean they are on board or owe this to you. Trying to analyze their behavior and their mind is a waste of time and energy. The more productive questions here are why are you putting yourself in the position of pursuing someone who isn't on the same page? What is that drive? Why does this feel like love to you? Does this remind you of a dynamic from your past? Someone with whom you needed to chase or impress to feel loved? By getting to know the depth and complexities of ourselves we can accept that others have a whole internal world of shit they too are trying to make sense of.

Humans are object-seeking creatures. In childhood we internalize our parents as objects in order to feel a sense of emotional safety and love so we can freely start to explore the world and grow. When we transition into an age where we can start to test out dating and romance, we learn to internalize partners to gain the same effect. What would love and partnership look like if we were taught to turn within first? To ground ourselves and find safety there before we seek another? To move our baseline away from the missteps of our parents to a sense of trust and stability in our identities, rather than placing this fragile ambiguous sense in the unsteady hands of others? Would heartbreak be less devastating? Could it become a sacred sanctuary of our own making that can easily be rearranged to fit a new furnishing and then returned to its original floor plan if the new object just doesn't fit like we thought?

Feeling grounded in exactly who the fuck you are is essential for reducing the confusion on what the fuck happened when things fall apart. This shift within yourself will also shift and influence the individuals you choose to build relationships with. You will feel more comfortable choosing yourself over another unhealthy dynamic just to not feel alone. Finally, when and if your heart does break, this deeper level of connection you have within will allow you to recover at a quicker rate. You can become your own internalized sense of love and safety. This is the needed baseline.

For the visual learners, I made this wormhole inspired diagram about the self-growth process:

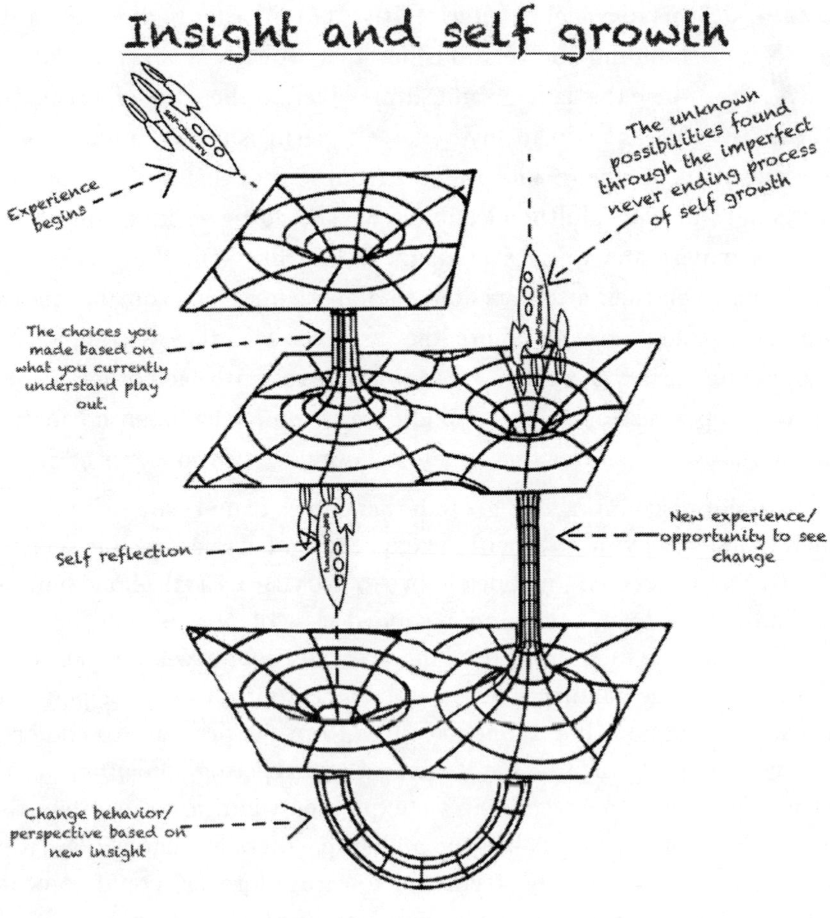

WHAT THE HELL DO I WANT?

This may feel counterintuitive, but in order to work towards building the relationships that work best for you and reduce the damage and shrapnel left in the wake of breakups, I want you to give yourself permission to think of only yourself for the moment. The pressure from society that we feel from the early stages of our adulthood tells us we should be seeking long-term forever partners and this leaves many feeling like something is wrong with them when their attempts don't end in the imagined romance movie montage. Breakups are not failure; they are just the nature of complex individual humans trying to build meaningful lives with each other. I want to give you permission to put a middle finger up to the heteronormative and oppressive structures that developed our society's concepts of love.

I am not discounting the growth that comes from relationships with others; rather, it's vital to what I am expressing. I argue that this societal construct and expected timeline of love to marriage is a falsehood built to keep individuals from having an expanded view of possibilities for their lives. It dissuades them from thinking critically about seeking their own joy, sans romantic partner. There can be much opportunity for play and curiosity throughout life if one feels free from the pressure to conform to an internalized norm. What if instead of expecting romantic love to last forever every time we feel it, we expressed wanting to maintain the relationship as long as it is healthy and all partners are happy? What if wanting to work on it long-term and towards "forever" could coincide with growing towards stability within ourselves?

It's rather interesting that we as a society not only perpetuate the rom-com love tropes of being young and in love but also accept "the awful marriage" to represent married life as we age. This is where partners resent each other, don't have sex, and play out this sadomasochistic dynamic as though it is the norm. Could this be different with a subtle shift in perspective? Could you feel freer to love knowing it's ok if it doesn't last?

Roles we play:

We all fall into "roles" quite easily and different people can bring out different roles we naturally fill. Sometimes it feels great at first, then it can be repetitive, like muscle memory; resentment you may have sitting within from an earlier experience starts to build and gets projected at your new love object. Can we bring this to our awareness without judgment? Recognize it for what it is and set realistic boundaries on what has felt bad in the past? If you're the caretaker, do you find yourself with people who enjoy or benefit from your care in ways that push you past your limits? Are you independent and never ask for help? Or dependent on others? Do you shoulder discomfort in order to maintain comfort for others? Are you passive, conflict avoidant, indecisive, get told you give "mixed signals"? Are you rigid in your ways and have trouble recognizing or understanding others' needs?

To have better breakups you have to understand yourself and the multifaceted thing we seek called love. Wherever and whatever you land on is valid, but it does not mean those you want to date will be on board. These things can also be fluid and change over time. You, the human that you are, are always in flux and your wants and needs from relationships will follow suit. Knowing where you are currently and being able to communicate this clearly and honestly to those you are romantic with will not only set up authentic clear expectations, but also make it evident early on in a dynamic (when the emotional investments are low) that those involved are or are not on the same page. The only thing we owe one another is radical honesty and sometimes that can hurt and cause disappointment and sadness. That's the risk we must accept.

The following section is meant to be a starting point for self reflection and how to understand the roles we play within different relationships. Not all questions will apply to you and there are many questions you may have for yourself that are not listed. This is meant to help you start to better articulate what you are currently seeking, what shifts you want to make within yourself, and what hopes you have for your future. Having a clear answer is equally as valid as not knowing or being unsure. Radical honesty with partners involves expressing what you do know and what you have yet to figure out. These types of conversations can help lead to a healthier ending if things do not feel like they are working down the line. The more people have the capacity to communicate the less acting out due to overwhelming emotional states will occur.

Reflection Questions:

Past Relationships:

- When you think about past partners, what patterns repeat?
- How do these patterns relate to relationships in your past or in your family dynamics? What do you think is their purpose?
- What patterns felt healthy? Where did you struggle?
- How can you improve as a partner? What have you learned about where you struggle and how can you do better by those you care about?
- What do you struggle with when it comes to communication? What effect did this have on past relationships?
- What have been major sources of conflict? What issues do you avoid, if any??
- What boundaries do you have and how do you articulate them?

Level of Commitment:

- When you think about yourself and how your life is currently, how do you see a partner fitting into it, if at all? What does a romantic relationship look like in your mind currently? Why?
- What does having a partner or pa? What influences do you feel shaped this idea?
- Do you have personal goals for yourself that you'd like to reach before you would be ready for a serious commitment? Why?
- What expectations, wants, and needs do you have from a partner at this time? Where do these come from? Which ones feel vital and which ones have room for compromise?
- What boundaries do you need respected? Boundaries are things you put in place to protect yourself and keep yourself safe, they are not used to control, manipulate, or coerce others into doing things. Ex:
    - **A boundary**: "I feel too anxious to be in a crowd tonight so I'm going to stay home but you have fun with your friends."
    - **Not a boundary**: "I get anxious and jealous when you talk to others so I want you to only talk to other people

when I'm with you."

- What needs do you have that a partner could aid in fulfilling? Emotional connection? Physical touch? Sex? A supportive ear? Fun and adventure? A sense of emotional safety and consistency? Do these needs align with the level of commitment you are seeking?
- What's your biggest fear when it comes to romantic love? Why?
- Are there religious/cultural/political/social views that would need to align? Why are these important to you?
- What qualities are important for your partner(s) to have? What are hard no's for you when it comes to qualities in potential partners? What feels vital?
- Do you have an example of a relationship you idealize? Parents? Friends? What about their relationships do you envy? Why?

Relationship structure preference:

- Monogamy is having one partner and typically involves boundaries of not dating or having sexual relationships with others. Does this fit with your idea of a relationship? Why or why not?
- If you fall outside monogamy, do you want a primary romantic partner and, with consent, others you are more casual with but also have a sexual relationship? Do these more casual relationships know that's how they are viewed?
- How can you make sure you and your partner(s) are understanding the dynamic in the same way? How can you and your partner(s) feel more secure? What would that entail?

Sexual needs:

- Is having sex a form of intimacy you are seeking?
- What makes you feel emotionally safe during sex?
- How do you ask and talk about cotnsent? How do you set boundaries for sex? * *Consent is ongoing and can be revoked at any time during sexual contact. If asked to stop, do so immediately.*
- How do you define what brings you pleasure? How can you talk to partners about their pleasure and how to increase yours, if

needed?

- Would you be open to trying new things expressed by a partner? What are things you would not want to do? Your personal sexual boundaries?
- If something occurs that makes you feel not valued or uncomfortable, what could you say to address this issue?

EVERYONE IS MESSY AND SO ARE YOU: HOW TO COMMUNICATE

There often seems to be a divide in this world between those who only accept things that fall clearly within a structure and those who prefer the abstract. Structure and the abstract are beautifully intertwined if you can learn to accept and see both. The structure of your romantic life resides within your wants, needs, and boundaries. The abstract is the unpredictable reality of emotions, experiences, and the actual playing out of the dynamics you enter with others. Most of us have been entering into relationships backwards, throwing paint onto canvas before we determine the size and shape of the frame. Falling in love with someone who has none of the same goals for their life can be devastating and feel like a betrayal.

Communication is key to not only maintaining a relationship but also to reduce harm if and when they come to an end. Radical honesty, clear intentions and boundaries, acceptance when someone says "not for me," understanding that someone can both love you and not want any of the things you do, and, even though it absolutely sucks, learning to walk away are all important to improving outcomes of your romantic life. The reason I brought in object relations theory was to allow you the opportunity to experience how complex and nuanced you and the way you relate to others are. To know this allows you to understand others as well.

All of the insight into yourself that you have gained should inform what you are currently seeking when it comes to relationships. Communication of these to others can feel scary but it's actually the only way to find others on the same page. People fear expressing what they want, because if it can't be met then they must deal with the reality of deciding how to proceed. Some also fear expressing their wants because it could cause an emotional response or turn into a conflict. Avoiding a difficult conversation out of fear can potentially cause more harm to your partner and/or yourself. A partner who feels they have been lied to or misled will be more hurt than one that was respected with honesty, even if what you have to say is something that they feel upset about. Staying in a relationship where your needs are not being met or one where you are trying to meet needs you are actually not interested in will only create a dynamic full of confusion and hurt no matter the side you're on.

We are all playing out patterns. For someone to show they are worthy of your trust they should show patterns of honest direct communication, their behavior should match what they tell you, they communicate without aggression, and they can deal with conflict without losing control. Being in conflict is actually a great time to see how healthy the dynamic is. Were you able to resolve the issue and feel safe? Positive patterns should be seen consistently over time, which allows for trust to build. If their patterns indicate that they are not true to their words, are flaky and inconsistent, or have bursts of behaviors that make you feel unsafe, you most likely will not see this change. People are who their patterns reveal them to be. The most charming individual cannot hide from the fact that their behavior does not live up to their hype. No one can get another human to change their behavior unless they want to. The only thing you can change is if you wish to continue pursuing them or not. A good rule to practice is this: *Address an issue with a partner, give benefit of the doubt, if you do not see attempts to change behavior and it continues to repeat, then this is just their pattern.* You must decide if this will be good for you or not.

Two perspectives, one phrase:

- *"People don't change"*—A person's patterns stay the same unless they are building insight and decide they want to shift them for themselves. You can never force insight or the want to change in another person.
- *"People don't change"*—What can appear as a sudden shift in personality isn't. They are actually probably just revealing another part of themselves you just haven't seen yet but it's always been there. You may not like it, definitely can't fix or change it, but what you do have control over is assessing if this is still a good and safe dynamic for you.

I see clients make the biggest shifts in their romantic lives once they get more confident in saying "nope, not for me" when it comes to dating. Learning to notice when something isn't right for you creates a butterfly effect because you start reducing the time spent on those who are not in alignment with what you want. You have more time and energy not only for yourself, but for those special people who are a "hell, yes!"

On the other hand, if you are not interested in dating someone, have lost interest, or are feeling ambivalent, it's best to just be clear about it.

Telling them directly may feel in the moment a potentially hurtful act but it is less harmful than disappearing, leaving them in a state of confusion, or becoming intentionally inconsistent in communication hoping they will lose interest themselves or "get the hint." In the romantic life quest that consumes our adulthood, you will make more friends with honesty and have a higher number of people resenting you with avoidance.

Feeling like there is something happening behind the scenes of a partner's life that one does not know or understand is one of the biggest anxiety producers. Take a pause, try to calm yourself down, look at the root of what's going on for you emotionally, and try to focus on the facts. Asking a direct question without inserting your perception can help reduce defensive responses. Getting an honest answer, even if it hurts your feelings, will relieve the anxiety of not knowing.

- If you feel confused, it's probably because they are being confusing.
- If something feels weird, it probably is weird.
- If you can't ask clarifying questions without them getting annoyed, angry, or any other emotions meant to get you to stop asking, that's the only answer you need. GTFO.

Hiding important information out of fear your partner will want to end the relationship is just as bad as lying. It will be detected as something being "off" so it's best to show your partner you respect them by being honest even if the relationship ends because of it. The assumptions that we make due to miscommunications and confusion are typically reflective of our own fears, not reality. Assumptions can lead to and cause conflict. If something feels confusing it's because it is, but that also does not mean it's the worst case scenario your mind is able to come up with. Just ask them about it. If you do not feel safe or comfortable asking your partner questions that in itself may be a problem to address.

If you are preparing to end a relationship it's best to just accept that it will be painful for all involved even if you're the one ending it. Plan for this. What can you do to reduce escalation into fighting? Think about the best environment to have this difficult conversation. Consider a time that could allow all involved to be upset without responsibility of work or kids to return to. Write out how best to express what you want to say to help organize your thoughts, reduce misinterpretation, and unintentional harm by editing the words you choose. Yelling, aggressive acts, name calling, and anything we grew up watching on *Jerry Springer* will just cause even more harm because they are abusive behaviors. Breaking up does not need to end in flames or property damage.

You and your partner are losing the individual with whom they had internalized for some time. Know it will be disorienting and trigger regressive behaviors. Plan for this. Don't text them every angry hurt filled thought but absolutely write these thoughts out for yourself. Sit on them for at least a day. Read them over and try to gain insight into what wounds are triggered by this loss. Rewrite it, repeat, maybe in a week of doing this you'll have a much more cohesive message that is less rooted in your initial regressed painful state.

Conflict does not have to be resolved in the heat of the moment. The notion that couples should never go to bed angry is out of an extreme anxiety of "what if one of us doesn't wake up?" You absolutely can sleep on conflict. The more emotionally charged the less either person is listening to the other or thinking clearly themselves. Breakups don't have to be one large blow out over hours. Take a pause, sit with yourself and your thoughts, plan to meet up again once the initial intensity calms. Breakups are painful enough, reducing the harm from words or actions done in anger and confusion is the kindest approach.

Take accountability for behavior that may have caused harm. Ask them to take accountability for behavior that caused you harm. This is one aspect of growing and learning from our relationships. Ask yourself: What can I learn from this? What felt good? What felt bad? What do I want to work on? What aspects can I look for in the future for red flags? What did my past partner have trouble with that made the dynamic unhealthy for me? Did I have patterns that created unhealthy situations? What can I shift for myself moving forward? It's not asking too much to want a healthy relationship with someone who wants the same things as you. With that knowledge comes the reality that not everyone you will want to be that partner will be, *and that is totally ok*. It's what makes our long term, lifelong, or forever partners so special.

Wanting a sense of closure is such a human-ass thing. Our brains want to understand the whole picture clearly and will crave details or create them to make the puzzle of the event complete. The reality is that I'm not sure we ever gain closure during the time we are frantically seeking it. It's something that can only come with time and distance.

Toxic positivity would tell you to *not cry because it's over but smile because it happened.* Fuck that. You can totally be sad, angry, and pessimistic until you're not. Any positivity or lesson we can take with us won't enter into awareness unless we allow ourselves to honor the painful experience of the breakup itself.

Not wanting contact doesn't have to be out of anger, but it also could be. Reducing or cutting contact can help with the reorienting phase as you start to make sense of your new reality and find a new daily routine. The most difficult part is removing them from being incorporated into your daily thoughts. Natural impulses to share something with them only to then remember the relationship has changed. Pick a close friend, tell them you will be sending them the things you would normally send to your ex.

CONCLUSION

Ultimately, each breakup is a loss that we have to grieve. The stages of grief that many are aware of were based on what it is like to be dying, not dealing with the death or loss of a loved one. No two grief processes are the same because no two relationships will be the same. The emotional response to the loss of a relationship is not just about the loss of love. The concept of your life's direction and sense of reality gets lost too. This leaves many feeling alone in their process.

Breakups absolutely suck, will suck, and continue to suck until one day it does a little less, then a little less, and slowly we can start to emerge from the pain and confusion. There are no clear steps to get through this grief. It's a wild ride through all the emotions that cause discomfort. The quickest way through is to fly direct. Feel all the feelings, cry when you need to, yell into pillows, write out angry emails you never send, ask friends to hug you when you need physical connection, be a mess, go dancing, buy plants, stay home and cry under your covers, order that article of clothing that will make you feel more like you. Think about your needs, try to identify what you can meet on your own, and what is appropriate to ask of your friends. Don't question or judge the emotions as they present themselves, you're going through enough already. The floor dropped out from under you, and you're freefalling until you're not. It won't make sense until it does, but being present through the painful ride after a breakup is the only way to draw a clear conclusion and complete the dissertation that was the lived experience. You are the raw data and the researcher. You are informing your future self on how best to proceed to improve the outcomes of the next trial.